Praise for *Dodge & Scramble*

"*Dodge & Scramble* has a view as large and open as the prairie and as steady as a row of corn. The people in these poems 'staked their lives on wind / and high plains,' and Morgan Grayce Willow tells us how and why they gave themselves to 'the one moment / that is enough.' In this book, we learn something true and beautiful about the children of the children of the Midwestern pioneers."

—Joyce Sutphen, Minnesota Poet Laureate, author, *First Words*

"What a delight to discover Morgan Grayce Willow's new book *Dodge & Scramble*. Here's a poet who dares to engage the reader in a world of farming and the land, then pushes the experience to the higher level of transformative myth. Every poem, every page demonstrates the thoughtfulness and grace of this insightful poet."

—Mary Swander, Iowa Poet Laureate, author, *Desert Pilgrim* and *Farmscape*

"Some poetry is poetry of memory and some is poetry of desire. Morgan Grayce Willow's wonderful collection, *Dodge & Scramble*, shows that poetry can be both. Many of the poems recall precise details of a farming life that has passed us by, but through memories emerge a childlike longing to 'unfreeze our desire/ for the perfect garden.' These are thoughtful, informed, and moving poems that should be on a reader's bookshelf next to Wendell Berry, Ted Kooser, and Mary Oliver."

–Jim Heynen, author, *The Fall of Alice K*

"In this splendid collection from Morgan Grayce Willow, America's rural midwest is draped in what can only be called grandeur—grit, cockleburs, and all. The landscapes presented here are often larger than life, and the passage of time geologic in scope—yet Willow never loses track of day-to-day amazements: a wayward billygoat, a Greek myth transplanted, a machine shed, a haymow or two. With *Dodge & Scramble*, the reader is visiting emotional and geographical territory both familiar and fragile—clearly a journey well worth taking."
—Marilyn L. Taylor, 2009-2010 Wisconsin Poet Laureate

"Morgan Grayce Willow celebrates our daily connections to agricultural cycles, grounded in seasons, community, and family. At once contemporary and historic, Willow creates vivid word pictures with quiet, unforgettable commentary. In clear-sighted verse, she returns to the family farm, lacing memory into the fabric of rural experience, including its beauties and challenges. All of us benefit from her vision."
—Denise Low, 2009-11 Kansas Poet Laureate, author, *Ghost Stories of the New West* and *Words of a Prairie Alchemist*

"Morgan Grayce Willow's elegies, blessings, and myths evoke not only the cultural time by which a family farm lives, but also the deeper time of the earth's geology, usually imperceptible due to our brevity. Reading these poems, I remember how our lands grow because of, as well us in spite of us, and will continue without us."
–Michael Walsh, author, *The Dirt Riddles*, Miller Williams Arkansas Poetry Prize Winner 2010

"With rhythmical sophistication, allusive richness, and precise figuration, Morgan Grayce Willow both invokes and evokes the spirit of America's heartland. Part elegy, part praise-song, *Dodge & Scramble* could only have been written by a poet whose profound connection to this landscape resonates 'deep in [her] cells.' Like Amy Clampitt before her, this is the muscular verse of 'an uprooted prairie-dweller.' And, like Willa Cather, another literary forebear, Willow's allegiance to those who labored, broke the sod, and planted their crops is made more powerful because it is rooted in the traditional touchstone of myth. In a world in which nature is always capricious, in which 'the indivisible / tapestry of seasons' shapes the soul, Willow summons up 'a disheveled history' so vivid that the reader cannot help but react viscerally to these poems as they open out and reflect our communal, human condition."

—Francine Sterle, author, *Nude in Winter*

"The Midwestern landscape, physical, social, political, is the foreground for the poems in *Dodge & Scramble*. Cornfields, silos, barns, far horizons are the stage upon which the poor players, farmers, families, daughters, live and act. It is honored, praised, worshiped, from the rhythm of horse hooves over gravel roads, to the sweeping flights of swallows under creek bridges, to the sentinel blackbirds returning to their towering cattails. In the tradition of Bill Holm and Robert Bly, Morgan Grayce Willow, in her deeply moving book, gives us a litany of poems so that we can chant our way to the barn and know exactly where we are singing."

–Walter Bargen, First Poet Laureate of Missouri

"Reading Morgan Grayce Willow's *Dodge & Scramble*, I'm reminded of the wisdom of objects, how the tools, utensils, and ornaments of our homes guide us through the days. Silently observing, they offer us wisdom when we need it and correction when we deserve it. This rich evocation of growing up on the farm, where the connections to plants, animals, and implements are primal, captures both a child's inherent sense of security and an adult's acquired determination to survive, as the parents 'dodge / and scramble yet one more year / to keep this land / in the family.' If you also spent childhood days on a farm, as I have, be prepared for sensory memories to come back in a rush. Full of barn cats, Holsteins, fallow fields, harmonicas, thunder and lightning, haymows, and laundry hung on a line to dry, these poems honor a way of life that is close to the land, where 'the seam at the edge of prairie and sky / lives deep in our cells,' and that unfolds in the thick of history, 'beneath wagons and graveyards / fanning across the breadbasket.' In Dodge & Scramble, Morgan Grayce Willow pays wise and worldly tribute to 'the workings of things.'"

—James Cihlar, author, *Rancho Nostalgia* and *Undoing*

"*Dodge & Scramble* is an evocative love song that weaves together place, time, memory in seasonal and human rhythms. Morgan Grayce Willow writes into the mystery of home, balancing how where we come from names us, with gentle precision and wide perspective. Her poems lead us to the origins of life visible in the details, such as in her poem 'Root Sutra,' in which she writes, 'O Root, perfect beauty, / wither us backward in time, / down and into the indivisible / tapestry of seasons./ Road out of history./ Tunnel to the afterlife.' She ends this lyrical collection with a poem aptly titled 'Blessing,' reminding us of 'the one moment / that is enough,' after a marvelous poetic

journey exploring how life composes such moments and composes us within and beyond such moments."
–Caryn Mirriam-Goldberg, 2011-2013 Kansas Poet Laureate, author, *The Divorce Girl: A Novel of Art and Soul*

"With the true poet's eye for specifics and detail—red fox, pink granite, the 'shining curve' of a ploughshare and 'toast buttered out to the very crust'—Morgan Grayce Willow names this mid-western landscape and its homesteaders—her ancestors—into existence and creates a sustained meditation on our human relationship to the land and its history. The landscape itself is a central figure here, but this is not a romanticised world: there is blood, and ruin, and the anguish of people caught between a longing for the countries they left behind and the hope embodied in the new land they have settled; a people who can never be 'indigenous' in a land that is 'the never-ours land / that we claimed our own.' And this is the legacy Willow has inherited and from which she writes: 'A disheveled history,' she claims, 'condenses here.' And it does, beautifully, by celebrating a culturally complex way of life and bearing witness to its erasure. Often elegiac in tone and always historically astute, *Dodge & Scramble* is a wonderful collection—a powerful mix of invocation and yearning."
–Jude Nutter, author, *I Wish I Had a Heart Like Yours Walt Whitman*

"In *Dodge & Scramble* Morgan Grayce Willow becomes the poet-cantor of the prairie. Who knew there was music in 'Sorghum and sugar beets. / Northrup King. DeKalb. / Archer Daniels Midland'? Through poetry Willow examines memory, place, and time set on the prairie, the essence of infinity. Willow intones, '...wither us backwards into time' and '...place / that remembers itself as marshland /and longs to return."

The poet goes about her job the way a hardscrabble farm kid might, working with details like buckets, buckles, gaskets, pigeons, fences, sows, winches, and nails. For help, Willow's imagination and craft let loose a cast of characters ranging from St. Isidore and Demeter to kids who swing like pendulums in haymows, to Gypsy crucifixion stories and what a thousand-year-old inch of soil knows. These splendid meditations and narratives are made of myth, history, survival, ecology, beauty, and desire for '...some trick of magic, / of dream or good sense, that can shape / the wilderness inside us into a better garden / than the one we've so longed to reenter.'"

—Sharon Chmielarz, *Love from the Yellowstone Trail*

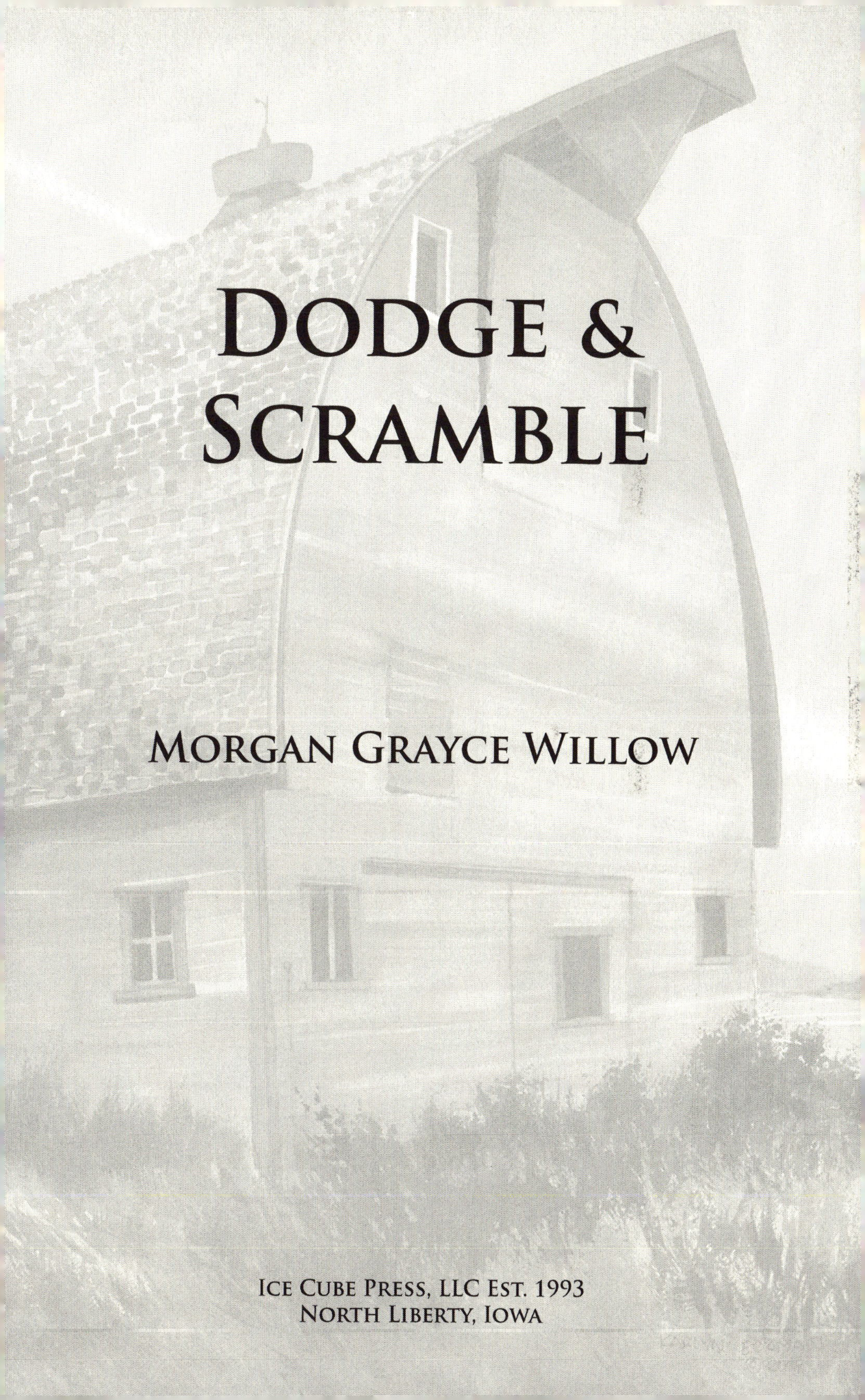

Dodge & Scramble

Morgan Grayce Willow

Ice Cube Press, LLC Est. 1993
North Liberty, Iowa

Dodge & Scramble

ISBN 9781888160734 1 3 5 7 9 8 6 4 2

Library of Congress Preassigned Number: 2013937026

Ice Cube Press, LLC (Est. 1993)
205 N. Front Street
North Liberty, Iowa 52317
w: www.icecubepress.com
e: steve@icecubepress.com
twitter: @icecubepress

The paper used in this publication meets the minimum requirements of the American National Standard for Information Sciences—Permanence of Paper for Printed Library Materials, ANSI Z39.48-1992.

Manufactured in the United States of America with recycled paper.

Artwork used for cover and title page: an original watercolor "Dodge and Scramble" by Karlyn Eckman © 2011 www.eckmanart.com

Author photo Rebecca Pavlenko, wordpress.rebeccapavlenko.com

For my parents,
Luvern and Ruby Weber,
who lived it.

Contents

I Dodge & Scramble

II Barn

III For Land's Sake

I

Dodge & Scramble

Plat

Meskwaki Indians passed along this creek.
Bobwhite were abundant then.
Yellow-headed blackbirds. Red fox.
Deer. Bison, even here.
An occasional arrowhead
tells this tale.

Swallows dip and dive
from mud-packed nests lodged
in the crease where concrete bridge-wall
meets ceiling, to the pooled waters
of the creek, chasing tadpoles
and the glint of light off minnows' sides.
Pink granite, tawny sandstone,
iron oxide and silicone
pebble the sand to tweed.
Over the bridge, crushed limestone
makes a road, marks the square mile,
a gravel grid that stakes a claim
on each quarter section.

In the northwest corner,
number eleven, footings
remain from the century-old barn
taken by storm, the homesteader's
chronicle: from hay racks to oat shocks,
from corn husks, to feeder pigs,

from dairy cattle, to the plowshare's
shining curve. From wooden-spoked
wagon wheels to rubber tires.
The return to iron lugs and buggy wheels
rolling on limestone
over the bridge, above the swallows.
The rhythm of horses' hooves.
The way to the meeting house.
The red-wings returning to cattails.

Farrow

You can see she didn't mean
for the little pigs to get out,
the seventeen Hampshires
scattered across the barnyard
while she stands, mittened hand
shading her eyes, in the open door
to the farrowing pens,
opposite the milking parlor.
She must be four, maybe five
in this photo, the old truck's shadow,
framing the right edge.
Nothing but gray in the sky
out to the left, though we know
fields spread beneath it
to the furthest horizon,
and beyond.
Even then the barn looked old,
vertical boards in need of paint
where wood meets concrete.
A broken sled leans
against the foundation.
At the window, one square in four
is broken.

She's too young
to understand the difference

between pork and pigs.
These are small enough
for her to squeeze tight,
if she can catch one,
wrap her short arms
around its belly, her smile
wide as its outraged squeal.
She's too young for the barn
to symbolize anything but home
for these curly-tailed, black
little pigs, the white band
around their shoulders
like the knitted scarf
tucked in her coat collar.

When, at noon, the voice
from the radio drones
prices per hundred-weight,
it's mere chatter to her,
though her dad,
who likes his toast buttered out
to the very crust, and her mom,
who dries her hands on an apron
made from last season's Easter dress,
contend with stacks of paper
in the corner: credit slips
from the feed store,
adding machine tape spilling
over tidy handwritten columns

of numbers, letters
from the bank. They dodge
and scramble yet one more year
to keep this land
in the family.

The coat she wears
in the picture is cut down
from one a cousin wore
in high school. The picture
doesn't show the jelly
on the kitchen table
made from grapes,
overgrown and wild,
climbing the grandmother's
windmill. The eggs at breakfast
gathered from hot nests of hens
the mother hates, her hands
scabbed by their meanness.
The bacon on the dad's plate crisped
to near burn, the way he likes it.
His shock when later
he rounds the corner
and sees hard cash,
loose and drifting
across the windswept yard,
squealing in pleasure to be out
under the cold April sun.

Root Sutra

Take the square root
of home, an infinite progression
of willow tangles
and corn stalks,
of soybeans grown for nitrogen.
Add shadow self of alfalfa and timothy,
of cocklebur and button weed,
the deep tug of royal Canadian thistle,
the white heart
of an Englishman's dandelion.
Break into the matted core
of early prairie.

Root, O my soul, dug out,
transplanted, water logged,
hung to dry, resurrected.
Bed for acorn.
Home to the makers of soil.
Propagator of forests
waiting for the fire of grasses.
Wind-defying net.
Breaker of stone.
Fascia beneath the planet's skin.

O Root, perfect beauty,
wither us backward in time,

down and into the indivisible
tapestry of seasons.
Road out of history.
Tunnel to the afterlife.

THE FRONT

I

We turn from one county road
onto another.
After we crest the rise
we see it, the wall
of deep charcoal,
a sharp demarcation,
as if an animated curve leapt
off the weatherman's map
onto the world before us.
It's headed our way.
Pieces of its frayed selvage swirl
along the creek bottom,
forcing willows, maples,
and the one black walnut beside the barn
to writhe, their limbs twisting upon themselves
as if seeking safety beneath their own
lower branches. Whiter sprigs of cloud
shapeshift against the whirling backdrop,
coiling, uncoiling.

We turn back.

By the time we get to the highway,
the torrent is on us.

You drive as one raised among these fields,
steering between lightning flashes
by instinct. I watch the right edge
where the roadway meets the ditch
just as I had from the back seat
when Dad drove through sleet,
Mom beside him, her jaw set tight.

II

All afternoon, we have wandered
the paths of our people. In towns
along the Minnesota-Iowa border,
where the largest populations
are in cemeteries, we've found
some of my German folks.
Some of yours, Dutch and Danes,
had been told to follow the Cedar
upriver to Austin, then head west
toward the stand of timber.
The place that would become Albert Lea.

Between ourselves and this lightning,
metal; beneath us, rubber on asphalt.
They had only canvas overhead,
wooden-spoked wheels held
by a thin rim of iron,
and a team of strong oxen,

more afraid of fire
than of rain.

III

The seam at the edge of prairie and sky
lives deep in our cells.
To see that line on a day like today,
undulating, its greens ranging from sharp,
mixed with yellow, to dull and silver-backed,
to see it tossed against that blue
by which all other blues are defined,
to see this interrupted by cumulus, white and occasional,
building and degrading to heather-gray,
then to gunmetal, now to near-perfect black,
to see it between light too shocking
for sight, to peer through this shield of rain,
this is to be backed into the elements
of our people's stories.

We go for high ground,
through water coming both down and up,
swirling around tires in this place
that remembers itself as marshland
and longs to return.

Nails

I

Every Passion Week,
I consider the nails
driven through palms
and feet, each slender bone
making way for the blunt
peg driven by a centurion,
with large mallet. Consider slow trickle
of blood, its drip
and dry into the crucifix,
sacred wood, since splintered,
scattered throughout the world,
sought after by knights and bishops.

O my God, I am heartily sorry
for each offense, of malice
or oversight.
I walk in the world on cautious feet,
yet still I step
on cracks.

II

Dad's thumbnail
bears a crack so permanent

that soil has begun to grow there,
lining him up
against history.

            Forgive
this thumb its trespasses.
It knows not what
it does.

III

Five thousand years ago Sumerians
made the first nails from bronze.
Romans used iron.
In the Colonies, 1777, someone
invented cold cutting.
Thus began the industrial age
of the nail.
            Mortise and tenon,
wood notched into wood,
gave way to the kiss
of metal against wood,
to the shrink and rust
of heat, cold and moisture.

IV

Mom sewed right through
her finger, the machine,

overdue for oil, stuck.
Or was she distracted by kids
who needed something,
had fallen and, this time,
were really hurt?

Point
in a new direction. She did
all she could.

V

There were to have been four
nails, but the centurions
drank up half the budget.
Three blacksmiths, one after another,
refused to forge nails for the crucifixion
of Yeshua ben Miriam.
Two of them were Jews.
Centurions set their beards ablaze
and pierced their sides with lances.
When the third, the Arab Khalil,
refused, they ran him through with lances.

Finally, they met a Gypsy
who had set up his forge outside
the city gates. They paid him the remaining
forty pieces of copper. Suddenly, after he had forged

three nails, the voices of the three dead blacksmiths
began calling, begging him to stop.
Frightened, the centurions ran,
taking with them the three completed nails.
The Gypsy, having been paid, finished
his work. The fourth nail, however,
refused to be cooled by water.

O Yeshua bin Miriam,
did you mean for Gypsies
to have to keep moving, to pull up
stakes and set the wagons rolling
every time the fourth nail appeared,
glowing and unstoppable, in every place
where they paused their wandering?
If at last, the fourth nail would accept
the sizzling, cool water, would your feet
unbind, would you step
down from the cross, would the Gypsies
find home?

VI

Like my mother before me,
I cannot grow nails.
No amount of gelatin
stirred into water, swallowed with breakfast,
grows them thick and strong.

So many gadgets
harm them:
                    seat belts,
aspirin bottles, price stickers,
cell phones, key rings,
pop-tops. Each thumb
is cracked deep to the quick,
covered with Band-Aids
or bound by glue,
blown dry with sacred breath.

          Praise calcium.
Praise protoplasm. Praise hardening molecules,
and the spin of atoms.
Praise all delicate ends
and the shields that grow
to protect them. Praise the chink
in the armor.

The Old Home Place

Wood siding peels from walls
of the old farm place,
blistered, stripped, shrunken.
Roof's aluminum sheets slipped
from puzzle-tightness,
irregular. All glass long gone.
The screen door twists,
crazy angle, its mesh drooping
like a heavy curtain.
Latticed light streams
through an upper window,
from beyond what once
was roof of what once
was home. Even in black
and white, rust shows
on barrels that held oil
to heat the stove that once warmed
a family. Here and there,
plaster sticks on slats
            of inner walls.

A disheveled history
condenses here, fresh pine planks
become dried, curled demise
inside the strict rectangle
of photograph. Trees,

visible through the one-time door ,
through walls, frame
the left corner of the house.
Even they seem done for. This
must be the second house,
replacing sod or chinked cabin,
just large enough to stake a claim,
built the year after
the barn was done. It must
have been white, with proper shingles,
though truss beams now
show through. The whole structure
settles in different planes,
what was once a parlor sliding
off and away from what once
            was kitchen.
After the family moved
into the third house, the one
with porch and hallway, this one
housed chickens, or maybe hogs.
The former kitchen became granary.
After frost heaved, the parlor
dropped, the kitchen rose up,
and time continued its foot-and-a-half wide
mark all the way
            to the roof.

At this point, I must believe
the family is in their fourth

house, a split level by design,
aluminum siding, possibly yellow,
a foundation extending well below
the frost line. Some of them
survived the drought years, the locusts,
the Great Depression. Others
the formidable sixties, Farm Aid,
the first Gulf War. The older ones
remember this place, while some
younger ones have surely returned
to this land, not just to burn off boards
and clear weeds, to cart away metal,
but to turn soil again, to plant
sweet corn and potatoes, to fill albums
with pictures of their house,
their garden, their chicken coop,
or fields of organic grain waving
through the history and wind
        of the old place.

One Thousand Years

Nothing but worms
and microbes, granite

crushed, not yet sand,
not yet soil. Pieces.

Then a leaf falls.
Another. Chlorophyll

makes its farewell.
Leaf after leaf

for one thousand years.
And roots of grasses

where tops mirror
the roiling of black-bellied

clouds as they travel
violently eastward.

Then worms, beetles, spiders,
enjoy the mess,

leave carcasses,
their spindly legs

added to leaf veins,
to grass roots,

netted firm
as a spider's web.

Add bark, singed,
the branch lightning's gift,

wood rotting and soft,
its inside now home

to larvae, cicadas,
locusts. Their habitat

dies. They die.
Soils born to breathe

even as Ezra leaves
for Europe,

roots filtering a network
deep, holding granules.

Sand, granite kiss,
leaf mold, bark rot,

bug wings, worm dung.
Add toads.

Add one pond water. Mosquitoes.
Add bats and swallows.

Add bison's weight.
Prairie dog dung.

Add red-winged blackbird
and meadowlark.

Rabbits. Eagles.
Deer. Before horses' hooves.

This inch. This black inch.
Well before the plow blade.

Before town.
Before railroad track.

Before World War.
Before the Russian Revolution.

Before the Middle Passage.
Before the Trail of Tears.

This inch. This black inch.
Before computers. Before shopping malls.

This black inch.
Before internal combustion.

Before the soybean
gave back its nitrogen.

Before anhydrous ammonia.
Before indoor plumbing.

This inch. This prairie inch,
the inches beneath

growing corn, squash,
and beans. Grow alien tomato.

Grow purple coneflower.
Chamomile, wild lettuce.

This inch and lambs quarters.
This inch and Canadian thistle.

This inch, the dandelion,
the starling. This inch

and dams. This inch
and tiling.

Before fences.
Up with the cribs,

aluminum, long and low.
Before silos,

brick, block and blue.
Before DDT.

Before crop dusting.
Before irrigation.

This inch before three-crop
rotation. Before

the futures market and trade
with Russia, with China.

Before global economy.
Before the value of the acre

fell. Before it went up
in the wind, this inch.

Before the river,
this inch traveling south.

This black inch,
bleached. This black inch

sickened and gray.
Sorghum and sugar beets.

Northrup King. DeKalb.
Archer Daniels Midland.

The tall grain towers.
The fallow fields.

The government's plan.
The family farm.

Hog producers, lagoons
of shit. This inch

percolating,
this toxic inch.

In creek beds.
In the water table.

This prized and damaged inch.
This one thousand year-old inch.

II

Barn

Iron Oxide

I have always been red,
joining green to blue
at the horizon,
essential as an axle,
turning the farm
through time.

Sky looms in the place
where I stood for nearly a century,
my shadows stretching
from my foundation
across the farmyard to the house,
then tucking inward,
doubling back toward the cattle pens,
and alfalfa fields, through the soybeans
and into corn.

I remember the slow layering
of shingle over shingle,
and the setting of the cupola
into the steep roof-ridge
when I settled into myself,
even before paint, the red
so bright they could see me
from anywhere:
the market, the church.

Up to the highest peak
under rain hood, red.
White trim on doors and windows
came later. Finally,
wheat dust and hay,
the smell of cows and swine,
a press of hooves,
the flat pat of cat paws.
Pigeons, too, their voices
quavering from the weathervane.
Swallows packing mud
into homes under eaves.
And humans coming and going
all day long.

Built for storing,
painted and repainted.
Redder than heart,
bright as blood.
I remember back to pine smell,
to boots climbing,
the prick of nails,
the beat of hammer.
The beginnings of shape
and story.

Spiders

They hold my aging together,
their sinew of daily weaving,
from the rafters to the cross beams,
the stanchions to the window panes,
every day a new latticework,
precise and fussy,
slung from the hoop to the backboard,
the ladder rung to the door frame.
This seining for food
softens corners.

I imagine myself
from the spider's eye,
my joints battered, the shingles flapping,
foundation cracked
at the joining of concrete and wood
where memory and the hay dust
collect:
   wagon tongues, oxen,
   canvas covers, ploughshares
   chipped by stone, swollen oak
   bursting rusty barrel-iron.
The dust hangs,
sticky and heavy,
   a truth like oats,
       and hay.

Prairie

When I was first built
tall grasses waved,
backed down off the wind,
then rose up in a dance
between air and earth.
Early in the season
the green, so new,
seemed to have gold
mixed in. There were
no rows, just patches
around homesteads.
Willows and cottonwoods
lined the creeks, snagged light
and tossed it back
in a silver-green sway,
  rise,
          and fall.
Shadows moved
across the surface,
pulling clouds along behind.

Then the cutting started.
Black shine came rolling
out from single bottom,
walk-behind plows. Hitched,
to a team: horses

in the good years,
mule or oxen in the bad.
From that to six-bottom iron,
forty-five mile an hour
tractors, to diesel fumes,
to the graying of the soil.

You don't notice it
at first. Then one day,
turns out it's not
the slant of light,
or the wash of memory.
The soil actually was
more black. It had a shine
that bounced up and back
like light off windows.
Was it too bright?

Who am I to say.
I'd have emptied and fallen down
long before now
if they hadn't invested big,
seeded from fencerow
to fencerow. Look.
            Now none
of those first grasses
remain. Not
  a single
            blade.

Corn Rows

One by one,
before they were even three,
he'd set them down
and say, "If you get lost,
just follow the corn row,
the one you're in.
Don't cross over.
The row you're in.
Take it all the way
out to the fence."

Out front in the yard
he'd point to the grove.
"That's north," he'd say.
"The barn here, that's east.
The barn is always east of the house.
The creek's behind us,
so that means south.
That don't change.
Same with the corn:
north-south; east-west."

At night, he'd work them
on the North Star and the Big Dipper;
daytime the sun's path.
"The shadow of the corn

never points south. Can't.
The sun is at its back."

Corn was check planted
in those days, wires
guiding the planter.
From any place you'd stand,
straight lines, up the hills,
straight lines down. Nowadays,
no fence rows. No lines.
No more north.

"Find your way to the barn,"
he used to say. "Then you'll know
exactly where you're at."

Foxtails

She'll sit there hour
after hour in the dirt,
pulling up one,
then another:
  pigweed, timothy,
  chamomile, clover,
  plantain, foxtail,
  wild potato vine.
She swirls them in the fine,
cool dust. She hums and sways.

    Everybody else
is working, the boys riding row
after long row on the Allis Chalmers,
yellow-green corn slicing hot day
into haze, cultivator blades
gouging out weeds.
Or walking bushy aisles
of blue-green soybeans,
pulling up volunteer corn.
Or baling – three times a summer,
in a good season – riding loose-kneed
on the rack, grappling bales
from the chute, one after the other,
smooth and regular as any machine,
their sweat and nostrils collecting
green dust.

She's getting out of this,
at the moment, making dolls
from weeds, twirling them.
She'll find out life's not
one grand ball. She'll be set to work:
gathering eggs,
picking beans, bringing clothes in
off the line, weeding row after row
of potatoes, onions, tomatoes.
Soon enough. But just now,
behind the corn crib,
those dusty skirts,
the dancing.

Haymow

I

My favorite time
is spring after the cows
go out to pasture.
Most of the hay is used up.
Cats hide their new litters
in cobwebby corners.
Pigeons and swallows
freshen nests.
The boys clear a space
for basketball, build forts,
circle their wagons.
Cavalry descends
to the rescue, bugled
through their small hands,
piercing dust motes
high among these rafters.

Everything's for play
after winter, before planting.
Unused haysling forks,
haul the rope and pulley,
the track and trip. Kids grab
the rope, climb the bale ledges,
higher and higher

to set up a long, slow swing.
They leap to the rope,
grab on with double-handed grip,
wrap their legs, brace their feet
on the end knot, and swing out,
widening the glide,
becoming pendulum.
Over the empty bay, back and forth
the arc narrowing with each pass
through hay-dusted air.

II

One boy, more than the others,
pushes to a steeper height,
a wider arc, a longer
slower ride, until once
he crashed hard against the granary wall.
Knocked him clean out.
The others scrambled
up the chasm, surrounded him,
the little ones crying already.
"Stand back," an older boy shouts.
"Give him room."
He slaps the kid a wallop that brings him to.
After he sits up and shakes his head,
the others run out for air.
"Don't tell Ma

or I'll whup you,"
he calls after them.

He'll grow up to other highjinks,
still chasing the wider glide
until he and his buddies,
go out drinking and driving,
fast, wanting faster,
until too fast for the curve.
He'll survive, but the spells
come on him after that,
a shaking and choking like to die.
He'll sleep it off
in the corner up here
beside the grain bin.

MACHINE SHED

Across the yard
in an open-sided building,
machines roost.
Whenever he's not in the fields,
he's there, tending:
  sharpening plow shares,
  oiling discs,
  changing tires,
  tightening pulleys and belts,
  fixing broken tongues
  on wagons and hayracks.
Tractors demand the most attention.
Valves and fuel pumps go bad.
Clutches work loose.
Bearings need repacking.

One winter he takes up
a correspondence course
in machine repair.
The mails bring packets
of parts lists, diagrams,
every piece of each machine
labeled, the inside back cover
a troubleshooting chart.
During the dark months,
he puzzles over

the workings of things.
Bookwork, he calls it.
The course binder thickening
until spring, then going dormant
as he struggles to translate schematics
from page to machine, from pencil
to grease under fingernails,
to wrenches that slip,
to bruised knuckles.

She plays nearby,
half in, half out
of the shed's open side,
her back in shade,
her fingers galloping
through sun-warmed dust.
The scent of grease and dirt
merge around her.
She jumps clear
when a wrench clatters
against an engine housing,
or a screwdriver slams
against the wall, her father
cursing the obstinacy of machines.
Later, the tractor engine idling,
she moves in close
to watch the see-through chamber
where gas courses through the filter's folds.

Broken parts accumulate in corners
faster than pages in the manual.
She asks their names – distributor,
radiator, clutch plate, coil.
Sometimes, holding the book
on her knees, she looks at pictures,
puzzles out the words. She knows
the little ones: and, in, the.
She presses her hand
over diagrams, tracing the maze
of lines out to the margin,
wanting the big ones, too:
            fuel line, spark plug,
            magneto, piston,
            differential, brake shoe,
            rocker arm.

Later, the tractor fixed,
he whistles an accompaniment
to the engine's timing.
She creeps back
into the patch of light
at the edge of the shed,
dancing the skirts of her weed dolls
to that tune,
raising dust.

Harmonica

He used to lean against the wall,
propped on a one-legged stool.
The milkers, hooked to cows,
chuffed out a bass line:
suck draw suck draw.
He'd reach then for the Honer
in an overall pocket,
start blowing those tune fragments.
His solos drifted all the way up
to ridgepole and rafters.
I'd feel my timbers ease at their mortises.
Cows would shift, one hoof to the other,
letting go the day's bad weather,
relaxing into machines
massaging milk from their teats.

Cats like the reedy voice
that oozes up through floor planking
into the hayloft, through what remains
of last year's harvest, neat stacks
collapsed by now into heaps as the tons
give way to winter feedings.
My relief becomes his burden.
He calculates feed costs,
grumbles, grows angrier.
He occasionally pounds the wall,

bruising knuckles that later
he'll wrap around the harmonica,
bending breath
into lonesome cowboy tunes.

Charmed, cats come down,
from the grain bins, from their hunt,
out from all their snug
lairs, their paws brushing
floor and ladder, their landings
raising puffs of hay dust.
They gather under his music
at the pan of milk he leaves them,
foam still warm from a cow's udder.
The old tom brushes one ankle,
winds round behind the other.
The man's shoulders relax a bit,
his right hand, steady
as an engine valve,
wavers out a melody.

One day he threw it.
Chipped cement off the wall
about head height. Didn't hurt me,
but halves of the harmonica
fell away from each other,
old and dry as peach pits.
He picked them up, hurled them
out to the manure pile.

He kicked the stool then,
as he strode through the tank room
out to the spring yard
where each broken machine
sagged at its specific angle
into mud.

QUEENIE

Twice a day the four-hooved
beasts get herded into stanchions,
same line-up every time.
The more docile among them
walk right up to the wooden bars
and wait for the man or his sons
to lock them in for milking.
The docile are never
the black-and-whites, those tall cows
who love to kick, jump fence,
who fight the hands
that relieve their swollen bags.
Some of these end up
wearing collars of wood
to keep them in.

The brown was never defiant,
sole Swiss among the Holsteins.
Something about her led him
to stroke her flank, slap her rump
softly with his large hand
as he set the stanchions.
Sometimes, when the others set him off,
he'd stand near the Swiss
till he calmed down.
I've seen many come and go,

and well before this man's time,
the breeds changing with the market: Guernseys,
Jerseys, Roans, each a little different,
this one special.

Kids felt it. She never kicked
when they pulled her tail.
She took the whole ear
when they hand-fed her corn,
never once grinding a finger
between teeth and jaws.
They'd even ride her, sneak up
when she was separated from the herd,
in heat or drying out.
They dragged bales beside her,
or made hand stirrups to climb up.
She'd turn her head to them,
then stay still, not even
swishing them with her tail.
On the silent Swiss, they rode
as if they were in the West,
and she were really moving.
When they'd grown taller,
too heavy, they were punished
if caught saddling her up,
playing Pony Express.

It started with a common case
of mastitis, one the vet couldn't heal.

She weakened until she collapsed
on her knees in the fresh straw
of the isolation pen. He had no choice,
by then, but to put her down.
Later, winch and chain
pulling her heavy brown carcass
onto the rendering truck,
he stood, shoulders slumped,
cap in hand,
despite the glaring sun.

What a relief to be just mortar,
bricks, and wood. Let him
note that absence twice each day
as he passes her stanchion.

Wind

Twice a week wash hangs out
by mid-morning, overalls pinned
between shirts, legs and arms
full up with breezes,
looking like boys astride the wind,
whooping up a wild bronco ride.
In spring, it's print dresses dancing
above dandelions, false flowers
greeting true.
It can be fierce,
that wind. It once seized
my weathervane, rattling the cupola.
Inside, pigeons tucked their small heads
under wings. Another time,
it nearly took the girl.

It was already dark, early.
The farmer had just gone inside.
I could see through a window
to the basement where first one sleeve
then the other went limp,
as he pulled arms out of coat.
I watched him bend to boot buckles,
straighten. Head held back,
he called to someone.
I couldn't hear his voice,

though I could see it
shape his face.

Then comes the girl,
brown coat half buttoned,
hat barely pulled over ears,
empty coal scuttle in each hand.
Everyone, no matter how small,
has chores: hers the trek
to the old brooder house,
buckets to fill with corncobs,
to stock up on tinder
for feeding the furnace.
Stretch by stretch, she carries
and stops, though the pails
are a full third her own height.

This night, wind seems bent
on hooking itself inside buckets,
dragging her back with each step
forward. She hunches down,
collects her air, then launches,
head sideways, into the northeast gale.
Beside the lightpole, it slams her down
inside the circle of light.
One bucket spins off. Leaves
and dead weeds skitter past.
Tin roof sheeting lifts, clangs down,

punctuates the bitch howl
of the wind.

It's not raining yet.
Wet on her face must be tears.
She looks toward house,
toward shed, now the nearer target.
Gathers her legs, one coal scuttle,
her breathe. She lunges for it.
Zigzags. Stumbles. Drops the pail.
Leans against the shed wall.
She reaches her chubby, ungloved hand
and lifts the latch. The bucket rolls off.
Door bangs open. She dodges inside.
Door slams.
Opens.
            Slams.

How to measure time.
Stars covered over.
Clouds deepest gray.
Leaves and dirt drifting
through the cone of light
beneath the pole.
The clang and slap
of tin on tin. Girl huddling.
Door slamming. Even to me
it felt long.

Finally, he calls from the door,
sending out her name.
Wind snatches it, west
over the house toward the next farm.
The door pulls shut.
The basement lights.
The sleeve of a jacket fills.
The door again. Hunched shoulders.
He pulls on a cap and leans,
trailing her name.
He crosses the yard,
snatches the loose bucket.
At the shed, he pulls the door to
and he enters.
When it opens,
first, a bucket, filled, then the man,
then girl, holding his other hand.

The trip to the house is swift,
almost too fast, wind pushing,
loosening tinder from the load.
She trips once. He slows
till she gets her feet.
Then they're at the house,
door opening, basement light,
again the arm retracting through sleeve.
He hangs her coat,
then carries tinder
round behind the furnace.

What I next see is a burst of chimney smoke
flattening under wind's pressure,
going low over the next farm, west.

Dust Motes

"See them, dancing in the light,"
she says. "Those specks
floating up, riding down?
They're really faeries,
elves and goblins."
The younger sister listens,
rapt. "At night,"
goes on the older sister,
"after the light is gone,
they come out and dance
in the dark."

Now the little sister cries.
"You're making things up,"
she wails. "I'm gonna tell."
She clambers onto pudgy legs,
crawls backward down
the steep haymow steps.
Next thing, she's running
across the yard. Then, pretty soon,
the mother out the back door, yelling.
"What are you trying to do?
You're scaring your sister half to death
with those wild stories."
She whacks the girl a good one.
"I catch you telling tales

like that again I'll slap you
till your mouth bleeds."
She turns back toward the house.

Now the older sister cries,
hides out in the dry and dust
of the hay loft, wiping her nose
on a sleeve. She didn't mean
to be mean. Soon enough,
she's outside, chasing
the big boys, challenging them
from the north grove.
"Bet I can go all the way
to the top and across."
She starts the climb up
an abandoned elevator winch,
her brothers after her,
her sister watching
from below.

Goat Kid

One day he brings a goat home.
Small critter, odd. First
I ever saw. Hoof split in two.
Hair coming out the chin.
Little horns sprouting
at the top of its head.
Didn't seem to know how
to stand still.

Farmer's wife was not too happy.
"Can't even milk the damned thing,"
she says. "They tell me
it eats Canadian thistle,"
he says. "It'll keep weeds down
in the north grove. I'm done
scything thistle."
"You keep that thing out
of my garden. That's all
I've got to say."

The dog got real curious
and real busy. Couldn't sniff,
nip, and dart fast enough.
The boys stood pointing
at the thing's tiny hooves,
passed the lead rope hand to hand,

then tested their theory
that goats will eat anything,
even cigarette butts.
The sister patted the critter's head,
rubbed its hard knobs
where horns had started up.
She and her dad led him to the grove,
tethered him. Brought hay, water, oats.
Then set to mending fence.

Not that it did much good.
The billy never stayed inside
anything: pasture, pen or corncrib.
Sharp-eyed jumper, efficient
as a deer, he found every gap
smaller than cow or sow,
leapt each new board,
every barbed wire strand.
Even electric didn't phase him.
The farmwoman glared at every escape,
each wave of destruction: lettuce,
onion tops, nasturtiums, hollyhocks.
The kid showed he would eat anything
and everything,
except Canadian thistle.

The cherry tree marked
her last straw. Four years,
burlap ball to roots and blooms,

its best harvest still to come,
she nurtured a vision,
just one fine thing,
some beauty to watch
out the kitchen window,
above her work.
Then in one dawn's light,
her tree seemed shrunk up,
its lovely form jagged and stripped.
She rounded the corner.
The goat leapt away,
cleared the asparagus bed,
then stopped and turned.
Glare met stare.

After that the goat got chained
to the dead oak tree,
its huge, white skeleton
heralding the border
between farmyard and field.
Buckets for oats and water.
The girl to keep them filled.
A circumference of defeat
ground bare within its reach.

Before the hard freeze,
a pickup pulls in the yard.
"He'll live by the Wapsipinicon,"
he tells the girl. "They got hills.

Can't grow a decent crop,
but they got a use for goats."
She leads the billy up the ramp,
onto the truck,
slips the rope from its neck.
"He won't need chained
in that hill country.
Guess I should have known."
They stand together,
watch the pickup's turning:
out the driveway, north,
on up the road.

North Door

I told the child
not to sit so close
to the edge, pudgy legs,
and dimpled knees,
at first just swinging
from my haymow door.
The north door, built
low for tossing hay
to cows below,
out finally in spring
air, the pastures not
green enough
to feed them.
She didn't
understand me.
Pigeons fussed
about their nests
in my cupola. They
were no help.

She watched swallows
packing mud, her black eyes
tracing blue-brown flash, those tails
twittering a webwork
of light.
I heard a voice

from inside: "Get over here,
outta' that door." I took it
to be a brother calling,
as a parent might have done,
though he was both
too young, and
    too late.

Sometimes
butterflies come
to that height early
in the year. Yellow
or white ones, airing
sticky wings, trying flight
for a first or second
time. Can't blame
the butterfly, girl's hand,
plump and reaching,
too far, and just
far enough
for earth to take
    over.

            The brother
found her. Dog ran
barking, then growling
to the gate, pressed itself
between posts, pawing ground
to get to its favorite charge,

brother screaming
from the door above.
            Worse, the farmer,
wrench still in hand, unbuckled
boot slipping
to the gate.

The dog got there
first. Sniffed, nudged her,
then tasted blood
where three-year-old head
hit corner of feed trough.
            The dog did all
that child's whimpering,
her eyes
mercifully closed
by the time the father
arrived.

Mourning Doves

Folks around here got
no time for that,
them birds up in the cupola
crying: *coah*
coo
          coo
                    coo.

They lose a lot of folks
to accidents,
combines taking whole arms
before anybody gets there
to shut the throttle down.
A shirt, maybe, wraps itself
around the drive train,
pulls them deeper
and deeper into the machine.
Eventually somebody
finds them. Never know who
it will be.

Funerals get scheduled
around milking and chore times.
Women hurry back
to get wash out on the line,
to get field hands fed,

every last one of them
expecting meat, potatoes,
and pie, doesn't matter
who got born, who died.
Work's got to be done,
when the field is ready,
when the sky is clear.

Once in a while, it's a fall
up here in the haymow,
or somebody getting bit
by a bee, some damn thing
always going on.
Back in the Depression
there was that one
hung himself.
That was one time
I wished I could talk,
or at least
get one of them pigeons
to carry a message,
make some use
out of that steady racket.
Instead, they go on
and on, like tinnitus,
a damned, unreachable itch.

Willow

It went down
like a parent gone mad,
branches and switches
tangling, weeping willow
smacking the wellhouse walls,
black cloud, green,
all one blur,
the old tree ending up
splayed out across the driveway,
wellhouse roof scattered,
broken pump standing there,
exposed. How I got by this one,
I'll never know.

Took a while for them
to get a new pump put in.
They milked by hand
till electricity came back,
cows bleating like they were tortured
instead of touched
by human hands.
Water they brought in
on a tank truck.

Then that girl comes home,
a couple days later, from wherever

she goes every summer,
crawls right out of the car
and under the skirt of shriveling leaves
around the fallen trunk,
the part not yet cut up and cleared.
You'd think she'd lost her mother
the way she carried on,
but the mother drags her out
long about sundown, the girl's face,
her clothes streaked with sawdust.

That's when they put up
the new pumphouse,
some modern kind of shed,
metal. House is white.
All the out-buildings, red,
same as me. Now they got that
smooth aqua building.
Don't much like
the look of it.

III

For Land's Sake

Patron Saint

At first it seems
the heavy, steady
beasts pull the plow
without a guiding hand,
as if inspired
by the very breath
of the soil,
the exhalation
of thousands
of earthworms
churning a miniature
mirror of the black earth
slowly curving
off the blade of the plow.
But Isidore knows
his angel tends
the oxen's trace,
clucks at them
with an airy tongue
when they veer off course,
taps them
with his stick,
a reed lent by the wind.

Isidore, meanwhile,
kneels before his Lord,

praying for rain
at the right season,
for strong seed,
for corn that will grow
taller than last year's,
its leaves even sharper-edged
as they give a whistle
to the wind's tune,
as they crackle in the hot night,
toward honeyed tassels,
toward ears
golden as the meadowlark.

Soil, he knows,
is nothing more
than a black meniscus
where the air passes
from the heaven below
to the one above.
Nothing less.

Bouclé

Imagine Demeter in her dotage now.
She's succumbed to Hades' terms.
The daughter tends her mother's ravings
for the part of the year she's here.
In her absence, cold fields
shoulder the sloping hill,
Persephone's mantle, furrowed,
speckled with tawny stubble
of corn stalks, a thin dusting of snow,
the clue she'd left for her wandering mother
who searched year after year,
venting her revenge on the earth.

Siblings at cross purposes,
Zeus gave in to his sister's pleading,
more annoyed than moved
by Demeter's excessive grieving,
the complaints from mortals
that corn could not be seeded
on barren ground
a minor annoyance.
Hermes, always eager to travel,
couldn't have cared less about the message,
or about the pomegranate seed
that confirmed Persephone's migration.

The old woman fusses the fabric,
first smoothing, then picking at the stubble
on the hills of her knees, slubbing
frozen soil until it warms and crumbles
beneath her arthritic fingers,
moistens and breaks apart
to take back the golden kernels.

The Up Close and the Far Away

Pick an object in a small town
museum, the metal seat, say,
from a single-bottom,
horse-drawn plow. Rust
will smudge your fingers,
your jeans pick up
long-waiting dust as you climb
into the seat. Or poke among
the rope pulleys and hay forks,
cracked-leather horse collars,
a massive yolk for a pair of oxen.
Imagine chest and shoulders, pressing
against the thick beam. Dolorous eyes
move you. Their widespread horns
frighten you, a little.
The ridge where skull bone
and horn meet: scratch there,
as you would a young calf,
its curly white forehead
an invitation to play, even though
this is an imaginary calf
in a past long
left to fancy.

    There is documentation,
of course, old newspapers

in another musty room, acid-scented
microfiche. There are bills of sale
from the stockyard long since closed,
records with carbon duplicates
whose perforated edge suggests
a buyer tucking his copy
in the pocket of a fleece-lined,
leather jacket as he climbs
in the Chevy pickup and eases
the clutch out slow
to avoid jolting the calves, their legs
already shaky from the giving way
of warm mother-scent to strange odors
of grease and metal.

Fact goes the way
of mildew and rust.
The particular remains.
Memory. Imagination.
One suffices
for the other.

Idyll

The trunk twists backward
where an oak leans over broken
wrought iron fence.
Mottled light stipples
through leftover russet leaves
onto the apron of acorns
blanketing a family of sunken graves.
They'd staked their lives on wind
and high plains, then lost their claim
against time.

Occupants in passing cars,
absorbed by speed
and the search for bars
on their cell phones,
miss the graveyard,
its refraction
of their own bright story.

For Land's Sake

A fibrous, root-fattened
hinterland of grass.
—Amy Clampitt

I

Calico dresses billow on lines across America's
fat mid-section, apron-pocket-pinned, rickrack rimmed.
Sheets snap. Heavy dungarees, sodden, hold

the lines down, inevitable draw toward a center
deep beneath the fat matted, worm-ridden carpet,
the mass of swaying greens: sage, kelly, tourmaline,

chartreuse, celadon, lime. Each a blade,
a leaf, a stem, a petal. Linked. Knotted. Twined.
Embedded. Hermes-roots, their message: hydrogen,

oxygen, nitrogen. In love with the zigzag
lightning. In love with mountainous thundercloud.
In love with the boom of hoof beat, pounding

pathways across and back, over
and back, millennia like this. Gophers, rabbits,
moles churning into it, carving out shelter.

Various by nature: big bluestem, foxtail,
buffalograss, prairie brome. Invasives
naturalized, tall fescue unrecognizable

to glaciers and moraines, to the seas
before them, to memory pressed
into limestone. Unrecognizable

even now to the paved highways,
computerized silos, to herds
of elk fenced in for trophy hunts.

Unrecognized by the billowing, lifting
shirts of farmers, waving on the line.
To a great grandfather. A grandfather. A father.

II

All summer long, except Sunday church,
we run barefoot in the lanes. Barefoot
to plant potato buds heel to toe.

Barefoot on the gravel. Only thistles penetrate
our toughened soles. Thistles, invaders
from Canada. Sparrows and dandelions

from England. Even earthworms, guests
brought by settlers to Virginia, become
essential to the family farm,

become our childhood lucky charm,
our toes splashing puddles of summer rain
among the washed-up earthworms.

This soil then, wet, deep, and settled
great grandfather to son,
till the Depression dries it up.

It's lost. Time passes. A grandson
buys it back. My father pressing
forehead into the cow's flank,

whistling to quiet her
as her last milk thrums from udder
to pail. Land bought, lost,

rebought. Sold. The never-ours land
that we claimed our own. The crumbling soil, the
not-same soil, pressed between fingers, testing

moisture. Watching the black go sandy, go gray,
searching for the earthworm in anhydrous-fattened
roots: "Monoculture

on the heels of slash
and burn."

III

Clouds of steam from the house's side
replace the billowing, rising blouses. Sheets
and overalls invisible.

Wind returns to power,
churning turbines for industry
and flickering blue screens

across the middle lands.
The planet struggles back
from the blade-cut, the plow,

its rout of thick, fibrous
root-fattened grasses
long since undulating

beneath the twin gods
of thunderclap and zigzag bolt.
Beneath the spread of prairie fire.

Beneath wagons and graveyards
fanning across the breadbasket.
Beneath concrete and fiber optics.

Better than fences the long rows'
genes. Better than soil
the alchemical brands.

Better than earth.
What need
            for land.

Massive Corduroy

the grassland shorn, overlaid with a grid,
unsealed, furrowed, harrowed and sown with immigrant grasses,
their massive corduroy, their wavering feltings embroidered
here and there by the scarlet shoulder patch of cannas

—Amy Clampitt

I

A velveting of language across the page,
a poet's progress, a childhood
in New Providence, Iowa,
same birds, same grasses and trees
as a place called New Haven.
How have I missed, for so long,
your syntax, your peculiar and lovely
use of the colon, your line breaks
like turning-ends of fields,
each corn row strict, weed free,
the turn-around coming just
where it must.

II

At age nine, you cried
in a window seat, an exile
like Jane Eyre, punished,
not as she by a stepmother-aunt,

but by separation of glass and rain
from beloved rose-breasted grosbeaks,
from pussy willows and oak trees,
from prairie grasses, who, like yourself,
are mostly immigrant. Like myself.
We are offshoots of one Great Revival
or another, unwitting purveyors
of the alien:
    alfalfa, dandelion,
    starling, sparrow.
The first team of oxen,
first Conestoga, the first deep
wagon rut, first sod-cut house,
first fire and brimstone sermon
in white clapboard church,
a small, empty tower, waiting years
for its bell to arrive from England
or Germany. Too many of us
have come to believe
that we are indigenous.

III

Even Eve's apple was hybrid,
or mere translation of fruit
ripped from Persephone's hand
by story tellers, by re-tellers.
Now I need you to tell me

which thread to tease
from "the raveled sleeve
of empire," to pull singly,
gently, to make way for a different
fiber. Or must the whole weave
undo itself, the entire tentshow of history,
collapse, before any good can come of it?

Suppose you pulled one thread;
I another. Suppose enough
of the children's children of pioneers
took up strands among rippling waves,
moved one quarter turn
counter clockwise, might
the untended wilderness reveal
a different story, unfreeze our desire
for the perfect garden,
break our backward, Orpheus-like gaze?
Perhaps nine-year-old you,
gazing through rain-streaked glass,
were onto something, some trick of magic,
of dream or good sense, that can shape
the wilderness inside us into a better garden
than the one we've so longed
to reenter.

Seasoning

Air above the corn field
is still, hangs heavy
with summer moisture,
rests against tassels
and in cottonwoods bordering the field
to the west and south.
Long twilight is earth's
one content moment in the day.
The sun's rays, interrupted
by a frame the leaves make,
edge time for us.
We could almost believe
it will do as we ask,
stand still for us. But just then
one, and another, then several, soon
an extravagance of fireflies blink,
each one lasting just long enough
for the eye to find
where it no longer is,
long enough to flavor the night
with light.

Blessing

Pink of the granite
meets gray.
In between
crystals shine.
Deep inside
a memory of fire.

The boulder lies
big as a cow
in the pasture.
The child
who climbs it
believes she's found
the very navel
of the world.

At the high end
of the huge stone
lies a basin
left by the great glacier.
In it, water
warmed by the sun.
She dips her fingertips.
She shakes this water
over the Canadian thistle,
the lambs' quarters

and wild oats
lapping the base
of the boulder.

Between water drops
and crystals,
between light that breaks
into color,
the one moment
that is enough.

NOTES

❦ "The Front" is for Cheri Register.

❦ "Nails" The story of the crucifixion of Yeshua ben Miriam and the Gypsy blacksmith is taken from Isabel Fonseca, *Bury Me Standing: The Gypsies and their Journey*, Vintage Books, 1995.

❦ "The Old Home Place" is inspired by a photo with the same title in *Rural Iowa Ruins* by Timothy C. Florer, Cumming, Iowa, 2002.

❦ "For Land's Sake." All quotes are from "The Prairie" in *The Collected Poems of Amy Clampitt*, Knopf, 1997.

❦ "Massive Corduroy" All quotes, and the poem's title, are from "Nothing Stays Put" in *The Collected Poems of Amy Clampitt, Knopf*, 1997. Some details of Clampitt's life are drawn from the introduction to that collection.

Acknowledgments

I thank the editors of the following publications in which some of these poems have appeared, sometimes in different form or with different titles:

The Heart of All That Is, Holy Cow! Press: "Corn Rows"
Water~Stone Review: "Root Sutra"
When We Become Weavers, Squares & Rebels Press:
"Seasoning," "North Door," "The Front."
Eclectica Magazine: "Idyll"
Low Down and Coming On, Red Dragonfly Press: "Farrow"
National Barn Alliance Newsletter: "Iron Oxide"
The Land Stewardship Letter. "Iron Oxide" "Corn Rows"

The poems "Harmonica," "Haymow," "Machine Shed," "Wind" and "North Door" appeared, in earlier versions, as a limited, fine press chapbook entitled *Barn Poems* created by Liz Tufte of Folio Bookworks in 2003. My thanks to Liz for honoring my poems with her beautiful bookcraft.

These poems were written and revised with support from a variety of residency and grant programs, including: New York Mills Arts Retreat, Lanesboro Residency Program, The Jerome Foundation, and the Minnesota State Arts Board Artist Initiative Program, funded, in part, by the Minnesota arts and cultural heritage fund as appropriated by the Minnesota State Legislature with money from the vote of the people of Minnesota on November 4, 2008. I am grateful to each of these programs and to the vision, hard work, and faith of the individuals affiliated with them.

I am blessed by the extensive Minnesota literary community and grateful to many individuals who make up the thriving and vibrant environment in which we all read, write, and make wonderful books. For their presence and support, among the many, I thank Kate Lynn Hibbard, Rondi Atkin, Naomi Cohn, Kathryn Kysar, Cheri Register, Sharon Chmielarz, Jude Nutter, Jen March, Michael Walsh, Barrie Jean Borich, Judith Katz, Ellen Lansky, Lynette D'Amico, Jeffrey Skemp, Matt Mauch, Michael Kiesow Moore, Heid Erdrich, Georgia Greeley, Leslie Faricy, Norton Stillman. And I must thank The Loft Literary Center for the many ways it and all its staff nurture this community.

The book is enriched by creative cross-fertilization. A very special thank you goes to Karlyn Eckman for borrowing a phrase from "Farrow" to name her exquisite barn watercolor. This exchange eventually led to a fresh title and the cover image for the book. I'm deeply grateful for permission to use the painting "Dodge and Scramble." I am further grateful to Steve Semken for his sharp design skills, which make the book such an attractive object, as well as for shaping a publishing process that's been a joy. My thanks also to Timothy C. Florer, whose photographs of rural Iowa both preserve and inspire. Likewise, thanks to Rebecca Pavlenko whose photography has graced numerous projects over the years.

I reserve the privileged final spot to offer gratitude to my parents, to my siblings and their families, to my cousins and friends who have all come up through the small family farm culture that spawned *Dodge & Scramble*. Many of you have known barns, too. And, of course, deep gratitude to Blake, whose support, so essential, endures.

photo ©Rebecca Pavleňko Photography

Morgan Grayce Willow grew up on a family farm in Mitchell County, Iowa, originally settled by her great grandfather in the 1890's. Her poetry collections include *Between* and *Silk: Meditations on T'ai-Chi Ch'uan*, as well as the chapbooks *The Maps are Words* and *Arpeggio of Appetite*. Her writing, in prose as well as poetry, has garnered awards from the Minnesota State Arts Board, the McKnight Foundation, the Jerome Foundation, and the Witter Bynner Foundation. Morgan's memoir "Riding Shotgun for Stanley Home Products" became the title piece in *Riding Shotgun: Women Write about Their Mothers* (Borealis Books). Other essays have appeared in *Water~Stone Review* and *Imagination & Place: Cartography*. A former sign language interpreter, Morgan published *Crossing that Bridge*, a guide for making literary events accessible to deaf audiences. She lives in Minneapolis and teaches at Minneapolis Community & Technical College, as well as The Loft Literary Center.

The Ice Cube Press began publishing in 1993 to focus on how to live with the natural world and to better understand how people can best live together in the communities they share and inhabit. Using the literary arts to explore life and experiences in the heartland of the United States we have been recognized by a number of well-known writers including: Gary Snyder, Gene Logsdon, Wes Jackson, William Pitt Root, Patricia Hampl, Greg Brown, Jim Harrison, Annie Dillard, Ken Burns, Kathleen Norris, Janisse Ray, Craig Lesley, Alison Deming, Richard Rhodes, Michael Pollan, and Barry Lopez. We've published a number of well-known authors including: Mary Swander, Jim Heynen, Mary Pipher, Paul Engle, William Stafford, James Hearst, Bill Holm, Connie Mutel, John T. Price, Carol Bly, Marvin Bell, Debra Marquart, Ted Kooser, Stephanie Mills, Bill McKibben, and Paul Gruchow. We have won several publishing awards over the last twenty years. Check out our books at our web site, join our facebook group, follow us on twitter, visit booksellers, museum shops, or any place you can find good books and discover why we continue striving to, "hear the other side."

Ice Cube Press, LLC (est. 1993)
205 North Front Street
North Liberty, Iowa 52317-9302
steve@icecubepress.com
twitter @icecubepress
www.icecubepress.com

scratching, scrabbling, dodging, then scrambling, and inventing
while putting the *good life* together with
Laura Lee & Fenna Marie

The type styles used are
Adobe JensenPro and TrajanPro.
Page layout is derived
through adaption
of the golden section/ratio.